WEIGHTS AND STUMBLING BLOCKS

THE NARROW ROAD

Jessica Bonita Thomas

WESTBOW
PRESS®
A DIVISION OF THOMAS NELSON
& ZONDERVAN

WestBow Press books may be ordered through booksellers or by contacting:

WestBow Press
A Division of Thomas Nelson & Zondervan
1663 Liberty Drive
Bloomington, IN 47403
www.westbowpress.com
1 (866) 928-1240

ISBN: 978-1-9736-4118-6 (sc)
ISBN: 978-1-9736-4117-9 (e)

Print information available on the last page.

WestBow Press rev. date: 04/03/2019

IN TIMES OF
LONELINESS

BINDING CHAINS

Self-hatred; feigned victory
Drawn to unwanted lust.
Dire hopes; sincere prayers
Earnest; in HIM I trust
Guilty tears; lonely heart
My soul's depth to ache
A slave is born; bound to return
All for satisfaction's sake
Hands of disdain; continuous flow
Not willing to cease the battle.
Blinded thoughts; vain moistness
Winds of guilt will rattle.
Wicked passion; glorious plea
Tyrannous rules of love
Only to free me; chains that bind
Through fire sent down from above.

GIVEN BY THE LORD JESUS
Written by Jessica B. Thomas
9 Feb. 1999

PLEASE REMEMBER ME

24 Sept. 2006

I thought YOU had forgotten me
And left me where I was
I felt YOU weren't there
or maybe overlooked me because

Everyone received their blessing
And I was left behind
And I was getting older
but it wasn't my time

I didn't want to settle
Trust that YOU'D still come
Inside my heart was hurting
And my faith was growing numb

I was told to "give it up."
My dream would not come true
I might as well forget it
GOD is not gonna do it for you

And when I thought to give up hope
And listen to the doubt
I heard YOU call my name
And say, "It's time to step out."

It was the perfect time
And the way was now prepared
If I had stepped too soon
It would have ended in despair.

Inspiration: Sometimes GOD will make it
uncomfortable for us so that HE can push
us into our destiny. HE knows that we wouldn't
Move on your own.

SUE'S DILEMMA

There once was a girl named Sue that was so lonely she didn't know what to do
So she asked GOD above to send her some love to keep her from feeling so blue.

She honestly thought she could wait, but felt GOD would be too late.
So she put on here skirt and decided to flirt on her own to pick up a date

Sue got in her car to drive and passed a fine man on the side
She asked him his name with no kinds of shame and decided to give him a ride.

Sue asked where he needed to go. He said, "Let's hang out! I don't know."
So they went to a spot, drop it like it was hot, and continued to go with the flow.

Sue felt she found her prey and asked if he wanted to stay.
Joe said, "Alright. We'll have a "Red Box" night with a nightcap to finish the date.

Sue decided that she would abstain, but the flex of his muscles brought pain, and
The shape of his lips caused her body to slip...for the rest of this part, use your brain!

Sue woke from her one-night-stand and knew that she lost her man.
The moment passed. Yet, the loneliness last, and an unknown problem was at hand.

She looked on her dresser to find Joe left a long letter behind with words that read all the things he said. Here are some of the lines:

"You're the one who wanted affection. You didn't ask for protection.
I thought you should know, to the "doc" you should go. I left you with an infection."

Sue dropped the letter in dread, for fear had rushed to her head...
For moments of pleasure she shared her treasure and she might even end up dead.

Sue fell on her knees to pray and asked GOD to take it away
She learned her lesson and won't fall to depression
But hope the test would turn out okay.

Gift given by the LORD JESUS
Written by Jessica B. Thomas
2003

THAT'S WHY

You felt alone so you picked up the phone
To call whomever you will
Friends of old; some nice, some cold
just to keep the heartache still

No one is there. It's not even fair
that you feel the way you do.
You begin to cry, but you dry your eyes
when you remember, GOD waits for you.

Amid the dissension, GOD gained your attention
since you never found time to pray
No time for HIS WORD, no preaching was heard
So, all distractions were taken away

You got on your knees and asked GOD, please
forgive you for putting HIM last
No wonder you hurt, you weren't alert
to the ONE who holds the present and past.

7 May 05
Written by Jessica Thomas

THE REASON THAT WE'RE HERE

You feel that your life is routine: you're born, you live and you die.
As a baby, you were pampered and comforted when you cried.
You became a curious toddler seeking many dangers.
"Don't you touch that iron!" "Be sure to stay away from strangers."
You aged to adolescence and many are rebellious
following the faddish crowd and making their parents nervous.
Then you attended college to expand your intellect
so that you can get a job for paying bills and writing checks.
Marriage and a family were your next consideration and
buying a fancy car and house took away many frustrations.
But what is your ultimate purpose in living this routine life?
You didn't find it in education, money, houses, husband or wife.
There seems to be something missing, and it's not riches, fortune or fame.
Those things were not fulfilling, they were just a part of life's game.
Therefore, I give you insight on the reason that we're here.
It's not for gaining riches, but to serve our LORD with fear.
We were made for GOD'S own pleasure, not just to live and die.
When you've gathered all your substance there's still an emptiness inside.
That emptiness needs JESUS. HE'S the ONE who will fill you up
HE can handle all your cares when you're drinking from life's cup.
We're here to make it home to our mansions from on high
For when JESUS says the word, kiss all your worldly gain goodbye.

Finished 13Dec1995

THOUGHTS AND FEELINGS

Why do I desire you, is the question I must ask?
After I received you will this strong desire pass?
My heart within me aches when I think you've passed me by.
I drowned within my pity; so, I bow my head and cry.
But GOD knows what I don't, and HE sees the storms ahead.
HE tries to keep me safe and away from all the dread.
HIS still small voice says "wait and I'LL reward you by and by.
Try not to be discouraged. Your reward will soon arrive."
So, I believe the LORD by faith, that HE heard my fervent prayer,
and I dry away the tears, because I know the LORDS aware.
I know that HE is coming, for now I've passed the test.
All along HIS only desire was to reward me with the best.

Influence: I was in love
With someone who didn't
Love me back.
Started 28 April 08
Finished 08 July 2008

YOUR mind IS ON ANOTHER

I remain, though you love another.
You hold *my* heart,
but *yours* is still with the other.
You pretend that you care,
but your mind isn't there.
I can feel in my soul,
another's love has your control.
So, I stand until you see
that real love lies in ME.
Just give ME a fair chance.
Let ME cut into your dance!
Though the other controls your flesh
I desire to give you the best.
You said that you two are through,
but it's written all over you.
And I feel left out in the cold
when I hear of your days of old.
Yet, I'm here 'til you open your eyes
and overcome the other one's lies.
I'm here until you finally see
that true love lies in ME!

Written by Jessica Thomas
Influence: I fell for a guy who wasn't
Over his ex-girlfriend. The poem is
Symbolic of JESUS speaking to us.
July 03, 2008

TEMPTATION

CONSUMED

Why should my happiness depend on your actions?
By the size of my world, you're just a small fraction.
I poured all my energy into pleasing only you.
I thought you felt the same or at least pretended to.
My mind was lost in you and it refused to stray,
Praying you'd be faithful or wouldn't go away.
I was making you an idol and didn't even know.
All I knew was where you were that's where I longed to go.
I'd cry if you weren't there and would think, "where could he be?
Is he looking for another that could take the place of me?"
I hated to feel that way, but it was hard to trust;
I know how other girls could be whose minds are filled with lust.
They'd ease their way before you until they win your stare and
then play the innocent role, but inside be fully aware.
Wouldn't care if you are taken or wear a ring on your left hand.
All they'd want would be your lovin' and to soon make you
their man.
Yet, I had to give you up, which was very hard to do,
because my mind was wrapped, twisted and entangled up with you.
Until I met the SAVIOUR who came to set my worries free.
JESUS showed HIS awesome power, how true loves supposed to be.
It was minus any hang-ups, envy, guilt and shame.
My heart skips a beat by just the mention of HIS name.
My happiness and joy now emanates from HIM!
And the more I realized it the more your grasp upon me
dimmed.

FIGHT THE FEELING!

So hard to resist the feeling,
but, if I do it'll quickly pass.
GOD knows how much I like him.
My strength is fading fast.
My intention is to fight it;
I know how things could go.
If he looks at me with passion,
my weaknesses will show.
It's so easy to give in;
so easy not to fight.
I'd find myself too far with him.
I know it wouldn't be right.
To keep my mind on GOD,
I must pray a fervent prayer
or fall into temptation,
and get trapped by Satan's snare.
GOD knows this is a battle
that I must decide to win,
because if I don't resist it
I will surely face it again.

Written by Jessica Thomas 2000?
Resisting temptation

I MIGHT AS WELL

I might as well, that is, give in
I've already halfway committed the sin.
So since I halfway committed the act,
no way my GOD would want me back.
My conscience is saying, "Stop now, there's time."
But the Spirit of lust is controlling my mind.
In the "heat of the moment" a feeling so strong.
"I might as well even though it's wrong."
Just a picture in mind, now I'm acting it out.
Never thought I would, but here I am, no doubt.
The guilt will come when this is done
but I block it out when indulgence has won.
It's like an addiction-give it up for a while.
But cravings return after the reconcile.
Here we go again! Like a merry-go-round,
it never will stop until the lever is down.
It goes faster and faster leaving no time to think;
a reprobated state-my mind is on the brink.
No more is it wrong-what a dangerous cost
to no longer think my soul is lost.
Time passes and I follow sin for more
that sin no longer pleases, so I cast it out the door!
and I move on down to a stronger sin.
If I keep on going death will win.
I know the deal but it's hard to flee.
I never thought it could happen to me.

I'm completely distracted from serving the LORD.
And I know that Hell will be my reward.
No Word in my heart-No weapon to fight.
I have served my flesh with all my might.
Though constantly warned I didn't take heed
That to serve my LORD JESUS is a definite need.
The roads so dark and I need the LIGHT
to light my path and make things right.
I hid it so long, thinking darkness covers sin but
I know the LIGHT (JESUS) is there
to be rekindled once again.

Thank you, JESUS
Given by the LORD
Written by Jessica B. Thomas
January 29, 1996

I'VE GOT TO HAVE HIM

You found your prey in church one day
Sitting all alone

Your heart just puttered your knees just shuttered
That seed of lust was sown

While the Teacher is teaching or the Preacher is preaching
You can't even concentrate

We bow our heads then a scripture is read
But your eyes only penetrate

He doesn't pay attention to your devious intentions
Of getting him to look your way

So you do all you can to better your plan
While all along you're straying away

Your skirt is higher and your top is lower
You're sitting really close to that man

While you're shouting, jumping, and purposely bumping
your knees are too close to his hands

During testimony service you make him nervous
Because you're leaning in too close

You've become so bold you've let the devil grab hold
And put a hindrance on your spiritual growth

After church is dismissed you give an extra hard twist
As you pass this gentleman's way

And you wait outside to ask him for a ride
As you're thinking of something to say

As he walks your way, you decide to pray
That he's willing to go along with your plan

But come to find out this man for CHRIST is sold out
And you didn't see the ring on his hand.

LURE OF SLEEP

When one sleeps
he's in a daze
Can't feel pain
in the deepest phase
Night will fall
he's not alert
Satan attacks
The soul is hurt
But GOD is there
to cease the fight
with quiet stillness
morning LIGHT
HE wakes the soul
to face the day
HIS brightness
scares the dark away

Written by
Jessica Thomas
May 2005

NOT AN AFFAIR BUT A SIN

It starts with slight attraction, but not upon your own demand
You know you shouldn't feel it. You wear a wedding ring on your hand.
Day by day you play it off, but you can't help but stare.
Before it was inconspicuously, but now you don't seem to care.
Now he is constantly on your mind and your spouse wants to know what's wrong.
So you say, "I don't know what you're talking about. I've been like this all along."
You are careful in your argument and your spouse knows something's not right.
You tell him that he is the crazy one and you'll sleep on the sofa tonight.
Satan paints a picture that so perfect to your eyes.
Your spouse is in the way, and your mind is filled with lies.
You try to gain the pity of the man who crossed your way.
He seems to know you **in and out** and has all the right words to say.
He treats you with respect; displays beauty both in and out.
So you invite him out to lunch to see what he's all about.
This becomes an ongoing thing, and you look forward to your dates.
Your spouse no longer waits up for you. You're always coming home late.
You make excuses on the holidays, claiming you have to work, but you're really with the other man, and your spouse has gone berserk.

Phone calls/hang-ups all through the night; getting mad if he answers the phone
You boldly date your lover, and wish your spouse would leave you alone.
You tell your lover your plan of putting your marriage away.
You rather be with him that you could love him every day.
But while you were out playing around, your spouse was on his knees
telling the LORD just how he felt with a heartfelt earnest plea.
You didn't care that his heart was torn; didn't care about his tears, but he went to the ONE who's been through it all, that comforted and held him near.
While you were unfaithful with the one on the side, he was faithful in walking the walk.
Though the neighbors even knew what was going on, he prayed no matter how much they talked.
One day you arrived at home to find (after boldly carrying on), your better half was nowhere to be found. He had packed his bags and gone.
Just as we were unfaithful to GOD by backsliding back to the world,
we thought it was better on the other side, when all along we carried the PEARL.

I was stationed in Albq., NM
And a friend of mine was
Going through infidelity.
Written 27 Mar. 1996

POSSESS MY REINS

I thought that I was over you,
you're constantly on my track.
I let you take control of me,
control of me; I lack.
Lifetimes filled with joy
our only visions far and gone.
Filled so with regret
I'm longing for the dawn.
Many have turned
against me,
one who strived to please.
I've become a clone to your
image,
paralyzed by your fatal
disease.
Paranoid someone is talking
destroying my own
self-worth.

Paranoid someone is
watching
that I'd cross the enemy's
turf.
If only I'd trust the SAVIOR,
the SAVIOR, oh, my SAVIOR
my only true deliverance
my JESUS, LORD and Savior.
To give in and let HIM
handle you,
you will set the snare.
Allowing me to go on with
life
as if you weren't there.
But still you tend to linger
so sure I soon would fall.
A plot to plan my breaking,
breaking, mind and all.

Written by Jessica Thomas
Gift given by the LORD JESUS
1998

SLICKER

Stop chasing the Devil! I don't care how fine he may be.
He doesn't believe in GOD! stop pursuing that Devil and flee.
He has your mind upset and he's playing the "hard to get" game.
He's luring you with his looks and with kindness just the same.
Satan has a plan and it is laid out just for you
to deter you away from GOD, using your weakest point to pursue.
He'd probably brag to GOD, "I'll make her come to me.
I know if I do or say the right thing, her conscious would surely
flee."
Satan will taunt and tease until you finally become his slave.
Before you know it you're blind again and acting just like the
unsaved.
A little bit here. A little bit there. You've now become addicted.
You felt that you could handle the test but continuously you're
convicted.
After he's pursued and conquered you and knows that he has
your mind,
he'll degrade you and make you feel like dirt for leaving JESUS
behind.
After convincing you there's nothing wrong in showing him
your love, and
you give him what he wants; trying to block out the LORD
above…
"You call yourself a Christian?" Is what he'll finally get to say.
"Yet, you were in your shame with me on this very day.

Get out of my sight! I don't want you. You're nothing to me but dirt."
But GOD is there to mend you again; to soothe your deepest hurt.

Thank you JESUS
written by Jessica Thomas
01 March 1996
influence: Satan wants to ruin our witness.
He's the accuser of the brethren.

TASK MASTER

Task Master trying to keep you blind
Keeping you blind til there's no more time
Not wanting you to hear the call of GOD
Keeping you in fear with satan's façade
Binding you up with webs of deceit
Webs of deceit wrapping as you sleep
Wearing you out til you lose your breath
Losing your breath til it leads to death
He covers the darkness with glitter and gold
Glitter and gold to lure your soul
Making you believe there's nothing more
Nothing more than what he has in store
When GOD has more than your mind can conceive
Your mind can conceive what you choose to believe

11.3.04
given by the LORD JESUS
written by J. Thomas

THE WRONG TREE

It's out there; the tree that's pleasant to the eyes,
It is a tree to be desired to make one wise.
Beautiful to look upon. A tree so ripe.
The fruit that grows upon it is just my type.
A fruit that the LORD commanded not to eat,
so appealing and alluring and to the taste so sweet.

Blessed is the man, who finds a good wife,
Who will stay by his side all the days of his life.
Not blessed is the woman, who finds a good man,
and tries to draw attention from the one she wants to land.
She has a "teenage" mindset of having a serious crush.
Every time she sees his face, her feelings turn to "mush."

The devil knows your weakness and will make it look so good.
You'd do anything to get him, break the rules if you could.
"This is a new day. There's no harm in asking him out.
That man will be flattered by your boldness, without a doubt.
Give him your telephone number and ask him for his own.
Set up a time that's good for him so you two could be alone."
That's what satan whispers, but GOD sees his intent.
So GOD says, "Wait on JESUS and I'D give you who was meant."
But you're in such a rush; there's no time for careful picking.
He doesn't have to believe in GOD- your biological clock is
ticking.

All things are possible with GOD so don't fall for that vicious lie!
Satan's trying to make you desperate so you can choose the wrong guy.
You'd soon regret your choice of taking the fruit anyway.
The pain would not be worth it, and the fantasy wouldn't pay.
So wait for the "tree of Life," don't take from the wrong tree!
Blessed are they who wait on the LORD! Trusting HIM is the key!

WAIT, SARAH!

Sarah, is a young woman filled with many passions.
Her desire is to follow CHRIST'S and walk in HIS fashion
She desired to get married and have children one day
as her biological clock steadily ticked away.
There were no men available as Sarah Jane searched.
They were married, too young, or too old at her church.

She mainly met men who were not into GOD
She'd invite them to church, but they'd feel really odd.
The time would come when the man wanted to play
But when Sarah said no he would quickly fade away
She was tired of the pattern that formed in her life,
and prayed to the LORD that she could be a wife.
Would she find him on an airplane, or maybe on a bus?
Would his name be Steve, Walter, Frank, Mike, or Gus?
What would he look like? How would he dress?
How would she know him? Would it all be a mess?

Sarah's been tempted in more ways than one.
Satan's toying with her feelings; playing her for fun.
He wants to tangle and spin her in his web until she's old.
Keep her in that cycle until she's worn out and cold.

But there's one thing the enemy failed to understand.
Sarah knows the MIGHTY ONE who holds the master plan.
All she had to do was surrender all her cares to the LORD
and HE'D send her the best husband as a suitable reward.
But Sarah grew desperate; didn't feel that she could wait
and chose her own man; felt GOD would be too late.

The beginning was filled with roses; lots of joy and glee,
but as time ticked away, Sarah's eyes began to see.
Her heart was feeling heavy, upset inside and hurt.
Her husband soon decided he didn't want to go to church
He cursed a lot, drank alcohol, and gambled away the rent.
Sarah asked the question why? he said, "Soon, I'll repent."
Sarah prayed to GOD, regretting what she'd done.
Instead of waiting on HIS blessing, she decided to jump the gun.
But because the LORD is gracious, HIS word is where HE stood.
HE took what Sarah did and turned it around for good.
Her husband began to wonder; asking questions about the Word.
He began to read the Bible to search for things he'd heard.
His heart became convicted for what the LORD did on the cross.
He repented and was sorry; knowing his soul was lost.

GOD, LIFE AND EVERYTHING ELSE

Bound in FREEDOM

I'm sold out to GOD, or am I sold out to man?
Thinking appearance is most important.
Let me help you understand!
My life belongs to Jesus.
HE was sent to set me free!
But you bind me with your chains,
because my skirts above my knee.
I tried to fit your standard
by letting down the hem,
so I conform to your tradition
to fit in with the rest of them.
But I walked into your church
and I noticed the funny stares,
because I didn't hide my shape
and they could see my underwear.
But that skirt is all I have
until I buy more clothes.
My financial situation
only GOD and I would know.
I noticed a lady coughing
and pretending she would choke.
She whispered to her neighbor
that my garments smell like smoke.
Even though I rode the bus
and I sat up front alone,
the cigarette smoke ignored the sign

that read *no smoking zone.*
Her eyes went to my shoes
and focused on my toes
her jaw dropped to the ground,
I didn't have on pantyhose.
Then she nearly fainted
when she looked upon my face
I wore a little makeup
but I applied it in good taste.
Next, they handed me a cloth
to wear upon my head,
and a sheet to wrap my legs
like a mummy when he's dead.
My sleeves were way too short
So, they wrapped me in a shawl-
gave me a cloth to wipe my makeup;
soap, water, towel and all.
They couldn't focus on the message.
They were busy scoping me.
And I couldn't help but wonder, "am I really free?"

Thank YOU, JESUS!
Written by Jessica Thomas 16 July 2006

DEATH SENTENCE

Your "coolness" won't cool you in hell!
Hell won't tolerate your choice to rebel.
Where the flame and worm never dies!
Hell won't cease just soothe your cry.
Your crime won't pay the bail,
when you're screaming in Satan's jail.
No mercy, no mercy at all,
when you ask for your one phone call.
No use in thinking of church
while getting your soul strip-searched.
It was nobody's fault but yours,
when CHRIST'S knock was ignored at your door.
Your friends were no longer there,
and couldn't be found anywhere,
when you stood before CHRIST at your end
no one could ever try to contend.

Written by Jessica Thomas
02 July 1999

ENOUGH IS ENOUGH

The circle of time returns so soon, a kaleidoscope swiftly rotating
Episodes of sin corrupt the course. The MASTERS evaluating
Glaring through the scarlet hourglass lies a heart's broken desire
Nursing the stream of pain that flows, snatching scarcely from
the fire
Rushing seas of ignorance, the answers ever surrounding
Waves of unacceptance; fruits of death are over abounding
GOD'S tarrying runs astray, few awaits HIS imminent descent
Drifting in gluttonous indulgence, though signs show subtle hints
Seasons repeatedly reborn, the harvest is gathered and tied
The sickle of judgment has glistened, robes of royalty set aside
Cherubim's stand for muster, instructions, and inspection
Missions all unsparing, and grace is undetected
Life's hands have reached their pinnacle, "Time will be no more!"
As the lightning flashes the east and observed by scores and scores
Ringing shout of an angel, trumpet gathers the sea.
Blinding through the clouds. royal fierceness, no more plea.

Influence: describing the day of the LORD
Inspired by JESUS
Written by Jessica Thomas
11.12.98

Feeding Itching Ears

Some yokes were on so tight,
satan pulled them out the door.
Your preaching should have loosed them,
but it tightened them even more.
Is the anointing there,
is all we want to know?
Did GOD call you to that place
or are you putting on a show?
You scratch their itching ears
with words that flow so smooth.
They're living as they please,
but soon you too are going to lose.
You preach like you're so great
as you gather earthly gain.
You worship filthy lucre and
disregard your future reign.
Can't even loose the strongholds,
because you focus on being "great."
Many are living in sin, but
you never set them straight.
You practice your dance in the mirror
so it could be down-packed.
Your preaching is humming and moaning
and you're putting on an act.
"That man can really preach,"
is what the people usually say.

But you never preach on Holiness
and JESUS making a way.
You're just a people-pleaser, but
it will surely come to an end
when you're standing in the judgment
answering JESUS for your sins.

Written by Jessica B. Thomas
Given by the LORD JESUS.
Jeremiah 23

FOOL FOR JESUS!

You ask what GOD has done for you but fill your life with grief?
You constantly complain because of doubt and unbelief.
You say you've only suffered, being often filled with pain,
and nothing ever comes your way but cloudy days and rain.
You say the wicked flourish as the righteous wither away.
And would it just be grand if you could live the other way?
You're at an all-time low thinking you should stray away,
but hold on until the end, dear one, the LORD wants you to stay.
What has Satan done for you but try to win you over
to the side that spoils you rotten and hangs you when it's over?
He deceives you to believe half-truths; taking over your mind,
to keep you bound in chains while you're waiting in death's line.
He blinds your mind to the future for instant gratification
so that even the very elect denies Godly edification.
Only to keep you from life; life in the Great Beyond,
to indulge in "temporal bliss" that dissolves when this world
is gone.
But GOD who's full of grace, invested HIS life in you,
that you can gain eternal rewards when this world is through.
So yes, sometimes you'll suffer walking in your doubt,
but having fun and riches is not what this life is about!
We're not just born to gain all we can just to leave it when we die.
Measuring greatness by riches is one of Satan's many lies.
You ask what GOD has done for you? Open your eyes and see!
The cross was not endured in vain, but that we would truly be free.

Written 18 May 1999
By Jessica Thomas
Walking with JESUS

FREE INDEED

So, you made a bad choice and you feel your life's a waist.
Half was spent in prison; the rest is caught up in the "chase".
Society treats you different; judging by your past.
Refused second chances, "rehab to outcast".
So, what's the use in trying when no one seems to care?
And your life can't be successful when support is never there.
But GOD is not like man who looks on what you've done,
but rather reads the heart and counts your sin as none.
So, get your house in order! Put all your trust in GOD
who promised not to leave, but guide with staff and rod.
Don't continue in iniquity, but live your life in peace.
For JESUS will exalt you in due season with increase.
Don't believe that you're a failure! Believe CHRIST set free!
You have a right to live your life! Through CHRIST there's victory.

Given by the LORD JESUS
Started 11 June 99 finished 13 June 99
Written by Jessica B. Thomas

FROM GOD TO ME, 2010
TESTS AND TRIALS

When you were lacking I
provided
And every time you called I
answered.
I stayed til your pain
subsided;
When the doctors said you
had cancer.

I loved you at your best,
though you ignored my every
plea
But it was just another test;
I had to know where you
stood with ME.

When you fell I caught you,
But your friends all turned
away.

I bandaged you up and
healed you
Then you turned and went
astray

Either you love me or you
don't
Mere words are not enough.
You will be faithful or you
won't
Not just when times get
rough.

You used ME in the storms
Just to keep you from the rain
But one day I won't perform
when you sleep in crimson
stain.

09/09/10
The LORD JESUS
was tempted in all areas.
HE was betrayed and is used by those
who only come to HIM when they're in
trouble

41

GAMIN' 4 LIFE

Playing on the court of life
You dribble through obstacles
Facing your ultimate goal
It is blocked and knocked
Back into the enemy's hand
Blinding and binding your way
You soon regain strength and
Return to your place
Leaping over boundaries
Into a slam-dunk of bliss
Where the ball of dreams
Explode into a shower of roses
for you.

Inspired by the LORD JESUS
Written by Jessica Thomas

GET READY

There lived man who preached, "The world's about to end!"
And no one chose to listen; they were indulging in their sin.
This man was building an arc and no one understood
What purpose it would serve; this contraption made of wood?
But he told them of a storm that was coming any day.
Though they laughed this man to scorn, he told them anyway.
"There's plenty of room for all!" Yet they refused to hear
and the more his heart grew weary. "The day is drawing near!"

One man said he would come, but he was addicted to his wine
The preacher said, "Come as you are, and you will be just fine."
He said, "I've got to have my women and that without a ring.
I just can't give them up right now. It's a 'manly' thing."

One lady wore the finest clothes. Everything was nice.
She said, "I have to have the best-can't make that sacrifice."
The preacher said, "Just come on board! Don't worry about the
rest!"
GOD will provide your every need. HE surely gives the best!"
She said, "I need my men. GOD in Heaven only knows.
I have to give them what they want so I *can* buy these fancy
clothes."

One said, "I don't believe you. It's never rained before.
I'll just wait to see the clouds, and then I'll enter through your door.
Every day's a normal day. There's no way you speak the truth.
GOD will never do such things. You haven't any proof."

Soon GOD commanded the preacher to board the finished arc.
"Don't worry about the others! Save your family from the dark!"
So, JESUS shut the door; sealed and locked them in.
The clouds began to form; the rainstorm and the wind.

The first man came and shouted, "OPEN UP THE DOOR!"
He quickly sobered up and didn't want to drink anymore.
His women couldn't help him. They were trying to enter too.
Then he knew there was no hope and there was nothing they
could do.

The stylish lady came and banged upon the door.
She screamed to him, "OKAY. I DON'T NEED THESE
THINGS ANYMORE."
Her men couldn't help though they offered all of their cash.
It wasn't any good. It was nothing more than trash.

The last returned and yelled, "I BELIEVE YOU NOW!
YOU CAN OPEN UP THE DOOR! I SEE THE PROOF IS IN
THE CLOUDS!"
Intellect couldn't save him, nor his disbelief and doubt.
For that day had surely come. No one else could help him out.

There lives a SAVIOUR named JESUS, who died for mankind's sins.
For another storm is "brewing" and it's time to enter in.
Enter the arc of JESUS while the time is right!
Don't wait until you see the proof! It is almost midnight.

2006
Written by Jessica Thomas
Gift given by the LORD JESUS

GOD

The GOD of the entire universe lives inside of me
The ONE who raised the dead and split the Red Sea.
GOD! Who directs the path of lightning in the sky,
made a way for us to live when HE
stretched HIS arms and died.
GOD, who walked the earth when Adam was in the garden;
GOD, who conquered death and granted us all a pardon;
GOD, who still works miracles and causes blind eyes to see,
is GOD who preached to prisoners and set the captives free.
GOD, who in HIS majesty and greatness reigns above,
is GOD who filled a wretch like me
with all of HIS power and love.
The clouds are the dust of HIS feet;
creation declares HE exists.
When praises go up in reverence to HIM
there HE stands in the midst.
GOD, who holds all power and victory in HIS hands,
GOD, who confounds the wise and
makes the simple understand;
GOD, who holds in HIS grip the heart of every king,
is GOD, the main subject in the lyrics HIS people sing.
GOD, who fights my battles! GOD, who hears my prayers!
GOD, the ROCK of ages, Rose of Sharon, always there!
GOD, a consuming fire! GOD, the light of the world!
GOD, the Alpha and Omega! HE'S the most precious pearl.
GOD, the humble Servant! GOD, the truest Friend!
GOD, who will never leave me but will
be there through the end.

HEALING

Feels like a calm in the midst of a storm
Like chills when it's freezing, because you're wrapped up and warm
Like a quietness in chaos or when troubled waters still.
A cool breeze in the summer or when a hungry person's filled
One moment there's tension and another there's peace
At times, there's emptiness and then increase
Feels like the sky on a moonlit beach
The stars are so bright they seem within reach
Like a mighty sunset overpowering storm clouds
With rays of royal violet; majestic and proud
Healing so wonderful, pleasant, and free
From the stripes of the SAVIOUR who suffered for me

Heaven or Hell

DARKNESS, BLINDNESS, FIRE, AND CHAINS
EMPTINESS, LONELINESS, HEARTACHE, AND PAIN
FRUSTRATION, DEPRIVATION, SEPARATION FROM GOD
DECEPTION, REJECTION, YOUR LIFE WAS ONLY FRAUD
PURE HATRED, NOTHING SACRED, THE WORM NEVER
DIES.
NO PLEASURES, NO FUN, NO MORE SUNRISE.
MANY FEARS, LOTS OF TEARS, ALWAYS ON THE RUN
PURE TORTURE, EVER FALLING, NO MORE THE
COOL ONE.
NO MANSIONS, NO MONEY, NO CARS, NO SWEETS,
NO FASHION, NO TRENDS, NO FRIENDS, JUST HEAT
NO BOOZE, NO BEER, NO SEX, AND DRUGS
HORRID SCREAMS, IT'S NOT A DREAM! NO KISSES, NO
HUGS.
EVER JOYFUL, TRIUMPHANT, HOLY AND FREE
BRIGHTNESS, ELATION, FULLNESS AND GLEE
COMFORT, SATISFACTION, EVERY DAY IN GOD'S
PRESENCE
SINGING, DANCING, AND GIVING GOD REVERENCE
TRUTH, ACCEPTANCE, AND REWARDS OVERFLOW
PEACE, HAPPINESS, AND MORE LOVE THAN WE KNOW.
UNITY, DEVOTION, REUNION, AND BLISS
THIS PLACE IN THE HEAVENS YOU DON'T WANT TO MISS

Given by the LORD JESUS
16 Feb 04
Written by Jessica Thomas

I'VE BEEN TOLD

It is said I must be born again and I really don't have a choice.
If I want to go to Heaven, I must hear the SAVIOUR'S voice.
Why is HE called SAVIOUR? HE saved mankind from Hell.
I can accept it or reject the fact CHRIST died because man fell.
I was told it doesn't matter if I believe in GOD or not.
One day I'll have to bow to HIM and stand upon my lot.
Why must I be born again? Why was a ransom paid?
Man was disobedient by a wrongful choice he made.
In order to regain life that was lost because of sin,
JESUS had to give HIS own to buy us back again.
HE still gives us free choice to accept the cross or die.
Don't be fooled by satan's trick to make the whole concept a lie
I'm ready to be born again and not because I fear.
I believe what JESUS did for me; my understanding's clear.

05.29.04
Inspired by JESUS CHRIST
Written by Jessica Thomas

IS IT ONLY WHEN WE NEED HIM

An empty church-A *full night club*
A gloomy altar-A bar filled pub

Three choir members-A full concert
Empty pews-So packed it hurts

Dead church members-Sunday's football approach
Weary preacher-Rowdy coach

Pretty low offering-Full slot machine
No support for the Pastor-More gambling "green."

No Sunday dress-A full wardrobe
Too tired for church-A nightclub "strobe"

No time to pray-A busy phone
Won't read the bible-magazines thrown

A free love meal-A full turnout
A piled up plate-A fired up shout

A needed blessing-Sore knees
No food on the table-A prayer's plead

A drastic disaster-A crowded church
A high death toll-A GODly search

Real close to death-Bibles read all day
Your soul is required-Plenty time to pray.

LET GOD

You said that you handed it
over
But it sits there in your heart
You were willing to pray
To give it away
But you didn't part

The reason why it's lingering,
the reason why I know
when something is said
Your face can be read
And the pain in your heart
will show.

You ask the LORD to help
Not knowing for sure what
to do

HE tells you to wait
He will never be late
Just allow HIM to guide you
through

Stand fast during the battle
Set your face like a flint
Leave it alone
For it's not your own
As the arrow of GOD is bent

Watch HIM defeat your
enemies
Rejoice while the fight begins.
Thank the LORD
For drawing HIS sword
And wait for the battle to end.

Given by the LORD
The day after I left
The church that I
Attended for 16 years
1.17.05

LURING YOUR SOUL

I'll be creepin', slippin' and easin' just to lure away your souls.
Sometimes, I'll be subtle and sly, other times extremely bold.

I'll ease into your church pretending JESUS is on my mind.
Satan has sent me in to assure your soul is left behind.

First, I'll hook the bait, cast it out to entice you in
and then I'll lure your mind as I pretend to be your friend.

I'll wait until the Word is preached to draw away your attention
and on the most important parts I'll cause all kinds of distractions.

Then you'll start to pull and the rod will start to bend.
When I know the time is right the reeling could begin.

Then I'll have you biting, because I'm such a brilliant thinker.
I have your soul in mind, so swallow hook, line and sinker!

I'll appear to you as light and maybe even darkness.
I'll have the most intelligence or maybe lack mental alertness.

Maybe I'll wear a suit and tie, fancy cufflinks and all.
Or maybe I'll be a bum; whatever it takes for you to fall.

I'll slowly reel you in while as my net patiently waits.
Until I steal your soul, I'll forever perpetrate.

Some may disengage! Others, I'll reel in all the way.
If you don't put JESUS first, your frying is on the way.

given by the LORD JESUS (7 Aug 1995)

OPEN YOUR EYES

You can't see in darkness.
You've turned away from light.
Life's choices stand before you
As you stumble through the night

Believing that you're happy
And that life is so secure.
You can't see the enemy, because
Your vision is obscured

You're feeling for life's answers
And tripping over time
Wrapped in satan's web that
He is spinning on your mind.

01.09.04
inspired by the LORD JESUS
written by Jessica Thomas

Out of The Mouth of A Sinner

You say that you're a Christian, but you're acting just like me.
So what's the use in coming to GOD when there's no change I see?
What's the meaning of backsliding when there's nothing to backslide to?
What did you repent from? I haven't got a clue.

You're hanging out at the nightclubs laying all up on the bars.
And even selling drugs on the side to pay for your fancy car.
You say you have the SPIRIT. Its sure not the one I know.
Your spirits are in a bag where *Jack Daniel's* name won't show.

You tried to tell me of JESUS with a cigarette in your hand,
Destroying your so called "temple of GOD" saying, "JESUS is the man!"
How do you expect me to hear you when I'm seeing your evil ways?
I might as well stay right where I am. Next to you, I'm already saved.

Your mouth is oh so foul, using words that cut so deep.
You say there's nothing wrong, but they make you look so cheap.
You have a way with words. I was tempted to believe you.
By the way your actions show, no way I'd really hear you.

Your stereo's blasting with songs that are less than pleasing to GOD.
When I listen to the lyrics, I can't help but think you're a fraud.

I don't think the LORD wants to hear a singer luring somebody to bed,
but you continue to play the tunes while bopping your mixed-up head.

You faithfully drive the boulevard picking up girls on the street...
Still satisfying the flesh, flirting with everyone you meet.
And you're telling me to repent? Now I really am confused.
You're calling me a sinner when you're the one who's running loose.

So before you tell of JESUS you need to get your own self straight!
And before you tell me I'm going to Hell, look at your own crooked fate!

Gift of writing given
by the LORD JESUS
written by Jessica B. Thomas
02 Sept. 1995

Pity Party

Break out the harps and the violins too!
Play a sad song to accompany you.
Tell them your story; bring them to tears
from the heartache and suffering you've endured the years!
Poke out your lip! Hold down your head!
Pause in the middle to make it sound sad!
Tell them that no one relates to your hurt!
You're the *only one* who's been drug through the dirt
Scope out the crowd, and find a kind face
that they would take pity and show you some grace!
Nobody's problems should matter but yours
for your trials always hold the highest score.
Make sure there's weeping and lots of tears,
especially when many have lent you their ears!
Tell them how nobody seems to care.
Family and friends can't be found anywhere.
Fall to your knees and ask, why you!
Why is your world so gloomy and blue?
Yet, as you fall further into your despair,
It's a slap in GOD'S face when you know HE'S there!
Until you wake up, GOD'S hands are tied!
You refuse to believe and your faith has died!
We all must suffer to gain our reward,
but remember our weapons are found in the LORD!

Started on 1.17.05 finished 4.22.05
Inspired by the LORD JESUS
written by Jessica Thomas

56

REALITY

I'm living in reality! My body belongs to me!
I can do whatever I want to it. My reason: living free.
If I want to have an abortion or fill my body with drugs,
if I want to sleep around or hang all night with thugs,
I'm living in reality! Don't preach to me with rules.
My body is *my* temple. You're the one who's being fooled.
You tell me that I'm wrong and my body belongs to GOD
and because I treat it freely, I'm the one who's acting odd.
You say that sin is glamorized. Don't give it other names!
And the way I use my words is just the devil's mind game.
You say abortion is murder and using drugs; addiction
And that sex is fornication and adultery is non-fiction.
See, reality, in other words, not living by GOD'S Word, is what
people use to justify the lies in which they've heard.
True reality lies in JESUS and what HE did for man.
HE sacrificed **HIS** Temple that we all may live again.
The day you stand in judgment, your "reality" you'll defend
You'll awake to true "reality" in eternity; in the end.

Given by the LORD JESUS
30 Sept. 2004/written by Jessica Thomas
Influence: We sometimes make light of sin to justify
Our own indulgence. The reality is, " sin is sin."

SIN

Next thing you know it's in your sight
Then it enters you mind and if you don't fight,
It lingers in place, Indwells your thoughts,
Consumes your time, and when you're caught
It brings the guilt, leaves the stains
Kills your spirit, replaces the chains
And if you waddle, you're covered in dirt
Then all can see and your soul is hurt
But GOD who knows and hates all sin
Yet loves your soul and cleanses again
Is willing and able with arms stretched wide
Wants you to know, HE'S still on your side
Just remember the altar, what HE did on the cross
And give up sin that you won't be lost.

SLOW DOWN

Young man running
Running a race
Too fast to slow down and
seek GOD'S face
Your mind is consumed
With pleasures unknown
Draining your soul til it's not
your own
Slavery chains
Dragging you down
Dragging you down to the
grave yard grounds
Warnings of love
To snatch you away
Yet you cast them aside and
continue to play

Refusing to hear
Your life is a lie
You'd rather give in
So forever you'll die
Visions and dreams
Are things of the past
You threw them away in the
devil's trash
He burns the visions
Torches the dreams
Regardless of tears
And your loved one's screams
It's your decision
To change your ways
Or remain a slave
For the rest of your days

10.22.04
Inspired by the LORD JESUS
written by Jessica Thomas

STAR

There's no security holding
me back
when I want to get close
to YOU
There's no one scanning my
words
when I ask YOU what to do
Even when crowds
surround YOU
YOU notice me standing
there
Squeezing my way within
Though I know YOU'RE
everywhere
I'm allowed to call YOUR
name
Without getting pushed away
And YOU answer when I call
And that without delay

YOU'RE not too good to dine
with me
Though YOU'RE the KING
of kings
YOU'RE filled with bliss and
royalty
And all the splendid things
All the riches belong to YOU
Yet, YOU walk among the
poor.
YOU know each and every
one of us
and we long to know YOU
more.
Though we tremble to
approach YOU,
YOUR arms will take us in
And YOU calm us with
assurance
As YOU call us YOUR dear
friends.

04.18.05
Inspired by the LORD JESUS
after going to Madea Goes to Jail
we wanted to go backstage, but
knew we wouldn't be allowed
to see Tyler Perry

THE STRONG SAINTS

I've been through the floods and I've been through the rain.
I've cried many tears with my heart filled with pain.
I've been through the fire; brought forth as pure gold.
Been talked about and spit upon, treated mean and cold.
I SHALL OVERCOME.
I've been through the wilderness; weak, ill and lame.
Sometimes I had to feel my way; still pressing just the same.
My so-called friends betrayed me when I needed them the most.
Sometimes it was even family who weren't very close.
I SHALL OVERCOME.
I've given my life completely to reach that glorious mark.
HE'S the cloud that leads by day and the fire when its dark.
I've learned to be the example to encourage younger saints.
I've learned to withstand the devil when he tried to make me faint.
I have a goal in mind. I'm not going to turn back now.
I have a made-up mind, for to GOD I made a vow.
I SHALL OVERCOME.
No weapon formed against me has ever been able to prevail.
For my GOD is the mighty SAVIOUR! In HIM I shall never fail
My pain didn't last forever and my trials all faded away.
Lessons I've learned through tribulations are testimonies to this day.
I've learned to call on JESUS who guides me by and by!
No one's ever seen the tears, but GOD has wiped them from my eyes.

I SHALL OVERCOME.

GOD'S moved a many mountains and casted them in the sea.

All because my faith has grown, HE'S done it just for me.

I didn't turn around when my heart was broke in two.

I didn't turn my back, for I know HE'S been there too.

I SHALL OVERCOME.

HE'S been there all my life and HE'LL be with me in death.

When my family left my side, HE was the strength that I had left.

I have lived to learn that my suffering's not in vain.

I'm preparing for eternity where my LORD will forever reign!

I HAVE OVERCOME!

THAT'S ME!

I see me in the gutter; walking the streets at night.
That's me who's hooked on drugs unable to do what's right.

The one who's down in the "dumps" unable to face the day,
is me who's at my lowest. Is GOD going to make a way?

The one that's cheating and stealing, that's me who's telling
the lies.
I'm the one who eats out of garbage cans to feed and keep her
children alive.

You see, I'm my sisters and brothers who can't find a way to cope,
and I'm to represent JESUS who died to give us hope.

So, when you pass their way, don't act like you don't see.
Extend your hand for JESUS and say, "I'm looking at me."

Given by the LORD JESUS
Written by Jessica B. Thomas
Finished 8 Aug 1996

THE FLESH SPEAKETH

Why can't you feed my
craving?
You know you want to taste.
Just a little bit won't hurt you.
Why let it go to waste?
Why go through all the pain?
Your desire's in your reach!
I'll respect you in the
morning.
　　(*Angry*)
JUST LISTEN AS I PREACH!
Before, you had a ball;
didn't care how much you took.
For some reason you abstain
But please, take another look.
For my sake, just reconsider.
I thought we were a team.
Temptation stands before me
　　(*Frustration*)
and it makes me WANT TO
SCREAM!
　　(*Subtly*)
I'm feeling kind of faint.

I'm beginning to get the
"shakes."
You refuse to quench my
longing,
Soon, I'm going to ache.
I'm not trying to hurt you,
Not even trying to rule.
I'm friendly. I won't
deceive you
or play you for a fool.
If I didn't know you,
I'd say there's someone new,
　　(*Feeling betrayed-
　　Hesitant*)
who formed a plan to kill me
That would leave just HIM
and you.
(*Back to reality*)
Anyway,
The more you disregard me,
The more I'll die away
Or fall under subjection but
Win or lose, I'm here to stay.

Gift given by JESUS CHRIST
To Jessica B. Thomas
6 Jan 2004

THINK ABOUT IT

If YOU love me, LORD why is there so much pain?
When I'm looking for the sunshine, why do I see rain?
I believe that love shouldn't hurt or cause me any sorrow.
I'm afraid to face the day, because I'm worried about tomorrow.

YOU tell me that YOU care, but why am I so down?
Why so much distress and it seems no hope around?
I couldn't feel YOUR presence in the time of storm.
And Yes, YOU said YOU love me even though I was conformed.

(GOD)
You're right. You are conformed to the world and its ways.
You ask, "where is the LORD?"
But, HIS word you won't obey.
You refuse to live in righteousness.
Yet, you want the LORD to hear.

HE loves you. Do you love HIM back or only when there's fear?
You seek HIM in your trouble or when you're feeling low,
When your credit is expired or when your cash no longer flows,
When your spouse decides to leave or when you're sick and nearly dead,
When someone's out to get you or when your children can't be fed,
When your sun no longer shines and your heart is full of hurt,
When someone's spreading lies, and has drug your name through dirt,
When your life has been required, and your pleading for your soul,
That's when you call on JESUS to place in your control.
But turn your life around instead of heading for the fall.
I can't say that you won't suffer but GOD delivers from it all.

Given by the LORD JESUS
Written by Jessica B. Thomas
26 July 2005

WAIT!

There's a prize
that's in disguise
if you decide to wait
upon the LORD
for your reward
that's not too soon or late.

It may seem
you've lost your dream
when waiting on the SAVIOUR.
But open you eyes
and realize
HE'LL answer without waiver.

Sometimes it may
seem there's delay
when there's no sign around.
You start to think
you're on the brink
and your blessings have been bound.

So, satan hands
you other plans
to hinder you from praying.
And you decide
to catch his ride
he says there's no delaying.

So, for a while
you wear a smile
indulging in your pleasure.
Then you see
Its "third degree".
Satan is "fair-weathered".

You then began
to pray again
thinking it's too late.
For you gave in
and didn't depend
on GOD who asked you to wait!

But GOD is true
and not like you
HIS mercies can't be matched.
So, to GOD you danced
for another chance
and HIS angels were dispatched.

GOD'S main concern,
you had to learn
to wait and pass the test.
Next time you'll see
just let GOD be!
HE only gives the best!

THANK YOU, Jesus
May 07, 1999

WE ARE LETTING THEM DIE!

People are dying in sin
not thinking that life has to end.
Boldly denying the LORD;
disregarding the Spiritual SWORD.
Hanging in satan's camp,
leaping bounds to receive his stamp.
Not caring what's after death.
Instead of right, they choose to go left.
We must work before it is dark
that the lost won't miss the mark.
There's urgency in the air.
Satan's workers are everywhere.
We need to prepare to fight
Stand up for what is right!
Speak boldly what's righteous and true.
For, saints, we have work to do!

Inspiration: Jennifer
and Lonell's brother died;
both without
the HOLY SPIRIT

WHAT HINDERED YOU

Remember when you were young
And on fire for the LORD
Didn't tolerate the enemy
You fought him with the Sword

Remember when you were happy
Not filled with guilt and shame
Your mind was filled with JESUS
And you proudly wore HIS name

What hindered you beloved
That you're no longer free
What pulled you off the course
Into the dark where you can't see

You've fallen from HIS glory
Back down into your sin
Your mind and hearts entangled
But GOD can mend it up again

You were so content
All you wanted was the LORD
Used to love to sing HIS praises
Lifting hymns on one accord

What happened to that fire
That burned so tall and bright

You were holding up the torch
Now it's dimmed from day to night

But let me tell you something
Get yourself on track
There's a calling on your life
That's why the devils on your back

Return to the ole' landmark
Where you first received GOD'S hand
Get back what satan's stolen
Stand up on GOD'S command!

04.10.04
Given by the LORD JESUS
written by Jessica Thomas

When They Shall Say Peace

Like a placid lake in a spring
afternoon
We are
Unaware of anything causing
ripples
When there are trees
surrounding our shore
waiting to loosen their leaves,
disturbing our peace

Like a cub in the bosom of its
mother
We are
Incapable of ever being
disturbed
until mother has to hunt for
our feed
leaving us vulnerable to the
beast
who continually roams our
camp

Waiting

So buried in false comfort
We are
Believing we are undefeatable
on our own
Until our lives are threatened
Looking to our own pride as
a shield
When it is carelessly held at
our side
leaving the center of life
vulnerable
Until we stand beneath the
BANNER!

Like a river flowing
peacefully
HE is.

03.30.03
Inspired by the LORD JESUS
Written by Jessica Thomas
Influence: Our Nation thinks
it its immune to terrorism
until 9-11

Where Ever HE Goes

HE leads me through rivers, bushes and weeds
where snakes like to hide and sin likes to breed.

Through smoke, darkness, and raging flames,
mountains, valleys, and rough terrains

Yet, the way is calm, and the roads are smooth
When I'm walking with JESUS I can't be moved

Inspired by the LORD
01.17.05-Apr.05
Written by Jessica Thomas

WISDOM

You must suffer to see
Die to grow
Sacrifice to gain
Live through to know
There's pain before healing
A storm before peace
Intelligence in ignorance
Lose for increase
Joy before mourning
Birth as one dies
Sorrow in laughter
Midnight then sunrise

Given by the LORD JESUS
Written by Jessica B. Thomas
Finished 28 May 1999

WORK WHILE IT IS DAY

People are dying in sin
over and over again.
Boldly denying the LORD,
disregarding the spiritual sword.
Hanging out in the devil's camp;
leaping bounds to receive his stamp.
Not caring what's after death.
Instead of right, they choose to go left.
We must work before it is dark,
that the lost will not miss the mark.
There's urgency in the air,
Satan's workers are everywhere.
We need to be ready to fight;
Standing up for what is right!
Speaking boldly was righteous and true.
For Saints, we have work to do!

Written by Jessica Thomas
Inspired by the work of the LORD
7 July, 1999

YOU SEE ME AS I AM

YOU saw me as a valiant soldier
When I thought I was a coward.
YOU knew that I could take on the world
As I took my "pity showers."
YOU saw through all the excuses
When I never thought I could.
YOU saw a tall brave warrior
Who handled the enemy like one should.
A leader of many nations, is how YOU called me out.
As I walked with "hung down" head
full of fear, uncertainty and doubt.
As I thought so small of myself,
YOU saw me as a King.
As I live each day, LORD,
YOU patiently make me
Into those thing.
I'm to never get puffed up,
I am just a tool YOU see?
And I am all these things for it is YOU (CHRIST)
Who lives through me.

Thank YOU, JESUS
Given by the LORD JESUS
6 May 96

YOU'RE NOT MISSING ANYTHING

Sometimes it hurts to live GOD'S way. You feel you're all alone.
Everyone else is partying while you're sitting there at home.

Your friends may ask you to come along to places you shouldn't go.
But you know it's not pleasing to GOD and you boldly tell them so.

You can't, you won't and you don't fit in for old things are passed away.
So, don't try to be like the "old-man," he's dead and castaway.

We are a peculiar people; to this world, we're not conformed.
For how would the "lost" tell us apart when we're hanging out in the "storm?"

Though we may have to shed a tear sometime, don't let it turn you back.
For GOD will repay you ten-fold for everything you thought you lacked!

Oh, there's joy unspeakable in living your life for the LORD.
But satan wants you to give up for you're closer than ever before.

Many will say you're being unreal and you're wasting your life away.

But I know that GOD really saved my soul and I give my life to repay.

So, don't you ever feel bad because of what the world is doing.
Don't ever let it bring you down for your day is surely coming.

Just know that JESUS is right there next time you're feeling down.
Put the devil under your feet as you stomp him to the ground.

Given by the LORD JESUS
Written by Jessica Thomas
14-17 July 1996 (I was 30 years old)
At a lonely time

THE FALL

FINAL BREATH

She sold her soul for you,
as you lured her with your charm.
For such a time as death
never what she wants to alarmed.
Once a lover of the LORD'S,
now eternally, she's lost
she was blinded by feigned words,
now forever pays the cost.
She put aside the HOLY SPIRIT,
blocking JESUS with her sin.
Every time she spoke repentance,
you would show yourself again.
Claiming you would soon come too,
but right then you wanted fun,
and once the time was right,
Denying JESUS would be done.
That day had never come,
and the final say was death.
All of your promises and planning
did not include her final breath.
Now the cycle starts again,
and you find somebody new.
Making promises to keep her
that she might falter too.
Trying to lure her out from JESUS
that you could have your way.

Trying to cover her with pleasure
so from GOD she soon would stray.
Claiming you would soon get saved,
but right then you wanted love
from the person you are after
and not the Godly source above.
But that person you are after
decided you're not worth her fate.
By the time you come to JESUS
another day may be too late.
That day may never come,
and the final say as death
and all of your promises and planning
will not include her final breath.

June 3, 1999
Influence: A woman who was in a backslidden state
died this morning of a massive heart attack

FROM DARKNESS TO LIGHT

In darkness, I denied YOU
I was blinded to YOUR LIGHT
I blocked out all YOUR goodness
Served the world with all my might.

I couldn't see before me
Didn't see the devil's trap
He placed it there to kill me
Couldn't see he had me wrapped.

His treasures lay before me
My flesh was feeling good.
I refused to even praise YOU,
Didn't even think I could.

It was dark, so I would stumble,
trip and tangle up in sin
but I continued on that path
though YOU were calling
for me then.

When YOU called me out of darkness,
I then could see YOUR LIGHT
I plainly saw the enemy
And I knew there'd be a fight.

I knew there'd be a struggle
And felt my life was through.
So, I began to close my eyes again
until I looked to YOU.

10 Jan 04

NEVER IN TOO DEEP

One day, there lived a girl; a lady of the night
who'd rather sell her body than to get her soul right.
She was always on the corner, always on the street.
The weather didn't matter: heat, cold or sleet.
She said, "I'm happy. I've been doing this so long.
It helps to feed my children, so how could it be wrong?
But sometimes there's an emptiness, and longing deep inside.
I'd feel ashamed and lonely, but I just cast those thoughts aside."
There was a man I knew who was addicted to his habit.
He'd smoke his life away and used his money to support it.
He used the rent money, car payment, and money for other bills
to satisfy his habit; though close to homeless, he felt fulfilled.
He said, "I'm happy. I've been doing this so long.
It fulfills all my desires, so how could it be wrong?
But sometimes I feel an emptiness and my heart is broke in two,
but I just cast those thoughts aside and continue what I do."
I met a man who indulged in "porn" to satisfy his lust;
T.V., computers, and magazines, is where he placed his trust.
He frequents all the strip bars; a regular in the clubs.
Every woman was an object of his "funny" kind of love.
He said, "I'm happy. I've been doing this so long.
It satisfies my feelings, so how could it be wrong?
But sometimes I feel a gloominess that makes me so ashamed,
but I just cast those thoughts aside and get back into the game."
I pointed out the emptiness these people felt inside
And told them of their MAKER who could cast it all aside.

If they'd only give HIM everything and break away from sin,
HE'D make their lives complete, just like "brand-new" again.
Though it seems to be so hard, since they've been doing it so long,
JESUS died to help them through, so how could HE be wrong?
What choice would they have, unless they want to die in sin?
They feel as if they're trapped; on nothing else they can depend.
Satan has their minds, bodies, and souls beneath his rule.
His chains on them are strongholds that makes them play his fool.
When they feel that emptiness, loneliness, and shame,
he presents them with false reasons not to call on JESUS' name.
He tells them there's no other way so he'll remain their guide
and they believe his lies and cast those other thoughts aside
until they reach life's end, where satan stands and laughs.
They're just other souls he's conquered that will surely face
GOD'S wrath.
Unless they give up all the ways that robs them of true life
and present their bodies to JESUS as a living sacrifice!

Given by the LORD JESUS
Written by Jessica Thomas
Started 1 Oct. 2003, ended 2 Oct. 2003.
Influence: A friend, Anthony Seward, who was going through
Guidance: ACTS Chapter 2, verse 38

LOOSE HIM

If I give him up I'll lose him
For I didn't let JESUS choose him
I prayed that GOD redeems him
GOD will, but he must believe HIM
Every day I try to persuade him
To accept the ONE who created him
But he'd rather disobey HIM
And serve who disarrays him
So, I said I must forget him
Let him go and let GOD fix him
Such a battle not to think of him
I know I'm on the brink with him
But in order for GOD to work on him
I'll back up so GOD can search him
If GOD happens to say I'm wrong for him
I'll rejoice for he now belongs to HIM
If he's for me, GOD can save him
No longer deny GOD, but will praise HIM
For GOD truly wants to abide in him
Then I can ascend to Heaven beside him.

Influence: I liked a man who
wasn't interested
In JESUS

SO FAR AWAY

I've traveled outside of GOD's
pathway
and journeyed down the road.
I dropped my cross of burden
to lighten up the load.
The reason why I wandered;
the reason why I strayed:
it seemed a whole lot easier
and many others walked that way.
I traveled down the path,
But the way became so dark.
When I turned around to look
I could no longer see the mark.
I ignored it for a while
until I came across a man
who tried to bind me up
and put chains upon my hands.
As I ran away I stumbled
and fell upon the ground.
I looked down at my feet
and saw that they were bound.

I was dragged through the dirt,
smothered in the mud,
covered up and filth,
tossed within the flood.
When all my strength was gone;
at the end of the path,
I was forced to stand up right
and face the enemy's wrath.
There was a force of wickedness,
envy, guile, and hate,
I turned to run away
though I knew it was too late.
But far off in the distance there
shown a tiny light.
It seemed so far away, yet so
radiant and bright;
and just when I looked down, and
my feet were about to give,
the LIGHT illuminated the
darkness
and I had strength again to live.

"Every bit of happiness
You can get, hold on to
It. Time is too short."
Aunt Dale
Written by Jessica Thomas
10/19/09
At a bad time in my journey

SPIRITUAL CHAINS

All mankind are born in chains after Adam and Eve chose not to abstain.
The keys of death the devil obtained, But CHRIST came to earth to remove the stain.

HE paid the price for the debt we owe.
Though some don't believe that satan's the foe.
He has them enslaved and they don't even know
that his trick is to have them and yet lie low.

His slavery will make you think you're fine.
It slowly but surely takes over your mind
Places a blindfold over your eyes that you can't see his tricks in disguise.

This slavery gradually lures you in.
It indulges your flesh in the form of sin.
It teases you until you slowly give in.

Before you know it, you're in chains again.
It's a cycle that slowly spins around.
It doesn't spin up; the direction is down.
The deeper you fall the tighter its wound.
And the faster it gets til' you hit death's ground.

It's extremely dark you will need the LIGHT
to pull you from wrong and place you in right.
Though the one who has you will put up a fight
The LORD will destroy him with power and might.

This slavery that has you that you can't see,
must bow down to JESUS and set you free.
The choice was given to you and me.
Slavery or freedom, which one will it be?

Given by the LORD JESUS
Written by Jessica B. Thomas, 19 Jan. 2004-Monday
Dedicated to my nephews Randy O'Neil and Ryan Thomas, with LOVE
We only want the best for you.

Straight Boldness

I thought that it was me
Yet, he drools in her presence;
bowing down to her;
leaving me in the trenches
waiting for my green to show.

I smile while thinking
who would replace him
when I take him to the pound?
When I have him fixed;
better yet, euthanized?
He who goes around sniffing,
so boldly that he'd bark in my presence.

As I smirk on the outside,
I grimace on the inside.
Showing myself in small ways
by belittling him in the middle of joy.
Acting as if I didn't realize
how much I hurt him.
Can he feel it? I hope so.

6 Feb. 2000
Disrespected by a boyfriend
Written by Jessica Thomas

THE PRODIGAL

I am a blackened light
gone dim on the city's Hill.
Letting you down, my LORD
though YOU forgave me at YOUR will.
The salt has lost its savor.
No more am I called a son.
After YOU placed your trust in me,
I still followed the wicked one.
This prodigal has not returned;
running swiftly to be in YOUR arms.
Leaving YOUR embrace numerous times;
I was lured by the enemy's charm.
Seduced by his gleaming demeanor
at a vulnerable time in life.
Knowing his schemes all along
I lay willingly under his knife.

Written after Meeting
M. Payne 18 June 1998
Dover AFB, DE

WHO ARE YOU HIDING FROM?

Who do you think you're fooling, perpetrating in the church?
With your skirt down to your ankles
and your collar so tight it hurts.

As soon as you leave the service, you're
right back in your mess;
talking all kinds of foul talk; wearing
your "bosom-tight" dress.

Calling your best friend's husband;
acting like nothing's wrong.
Meddling in their business where you know you don't belong.

You're nothing but a counterfeit playing the church-girl role,
trying to show some innocence when
there's danger in your soul.

Calling up your boyfriend; making sure he visits late,
so the neighbors won't notice and you
can "get some" on your date.

Rest assured, what's done in darkness is always seen in light.
No need to hide from people. It's with
GOD you must be right.

2003

WHY DOES SHE REMAIN?

Why does she stay there and put up with his lies?
Why does she wear shades to cover her black eye?

He tells her that he's sorry; didn't mean to knock her down.
She believes him and complies as she stands for another round.

She accepts his candy kisses as he holds her in his arms.
Just long enough to calm her with his debonair and charm.

Her family always warns her, but she chooses not to hear.
His words are so convincing when he justifies her fear.

Her self-esteem diminishes, as she becomes his slave.
She thinks no one would want her if she went about her way.

Though her family sees the light (for they see him as he is),
her mind remains yet blinded because the chains on her are his.

Why does she remain, you ask, when you know she's bound to lose?
Just take a closer look, because we all were in her shoes.

Satan won our pity then he knocked us down again.
We believed him and complied because we thought he was a friend.

We loved his candy kisses as he held us in his arm.
Just long enough to fool us with his debonair and charm.

93

The saints of GOD would warn us, but we refused to hear.
Satan's threats were so convincing. He tormented us with fear

Our self-esteem diminished, as we became his slave.
We thought GOD wouldn't want us by the way we had behaved.

Though JESUS is the LIGHT and sees the devil as he is,
some minds remain yet blinded because the chains on them
are his.

GIVEN BY THE LORD JESUS
INFLUENCE: CHELA
WRITTEN BY *Jessica B. Thomas*
1 Sept. 2005

RESTORATION

Don't Delay!

After you've conquered the game
and sought after peace;
when your health has declined,
and your age has increased.
What was the purpose?
What did you gain,
but a memory of all the goodness and pain.

Yet, there's more to acquire,
but you failed to see.
You neglected to try,
So, you have misery.
But it's not too late
if you're reading this now.
The LORD GOD is waiting!
we all must bow!
(ACTS 2: 38)

Thank YOU, JESUS!
Written 4/14/2018
while resting/sitting the bench
at Fort Monroe. Beautiful day!

You can't look from the outside
in, believing only what you see
and perceive.
GOD looks on the heart

I FEEL FOR YOU!

I used to feel for you
Now I don't.
My heart would ache for you
Now it won't.
I had the "blinders" on
Back in time
To all the games you played
With my mind.
My flesh would long for you.
It was in pain.
The guilt followed me
Cause I abstained.
You said you understood
When I said no.
Yet, you toyed with me
Just like the foe.
All the signs would show
When you would lie
And though my instincts warned,
I denied.
I used to bring up GOD
And you would choke
Though you knew
We were unequally yoked.
When your true colors shown,
I was shocked.

Your pitchfork and horns
Were initially blocked.
GOD rescued me
From your trap
For my eyes couldn't see
That I was wrapped.
I took a stand.
You were mad.
My GOD defended me
I was glad…cause,
I used to feel for you.
Now I don't.
My heart would ache for you.
Now it won't.
I had the "blinders" on
Back in time
To all the games you used to play
With my mind.

HE MADE THE HEARTACHE GO!

It doesn't hurt me anymore,
WHAT used to break my heart,
WHAT used to make me cry,
WHAT made the joy depart.

It didn't take much time,
WHEN I gave it to the LORD.
WHEN I gave HIM all the hurt.
WHEN I drew the Spirit's sword.

All because of GOD,
WHO removed me from that place,
WHO restored me with HIS love,
WHO saved me by HIS grace.

HE placed me on a ROCK
WHERE I no longer die.
WHERE the devil can't reach
WHERE his arrows can't fly.

I guess I'll never know
WHY JESUS loves me so;
WHY HE chose to pull me out;
WHY HE made the heartache go.

HE Saved Me

I was dying
I'm not lying
but was drowning in the sea
In the ocean
Much commotion
Waves of sin had covered me
I was worn
My soul was torn
as I fought to catch my breath
but from a boat
there came a float
Just to save my soul from death

Inspired by JESUS
Written by Jessica Thomas

HE TOOK ME BACK

Oh, the lies I told
And the mess I made
The goods I stole
The way I behaved
The hearts I broke
The money I used
The people I joked
The drugs I abused

Talked all night
Burned up the phone
Denied the right
My comfort zone

Out at the clubs
the gin and juice

Faked the love
Danced real loose

A vicious season
It proved to be
My flesh was the reason
I wasn't free

Oh, the guilt I felt when living
wrong
The hand life dealt
The "hard Knock" songs
No love/fake friends
Truly, I lacked
Yet, after all my sins
GOD took me back

Inspired by the LORD JESUS
Written by Jessica Thomas
Influence: a testimony was
Heard on the 700 club about
An x-Islam believer who
Converted to Christianity
And backslid for 12 years
His words: "HE took me back"

I DON'T KNOW WHAT TO DO

Heartache is like a river
gusting on the inside
tossed about with fervor
like a roller coaster ride.
In the pit of my belly
when my heart is broke
in two;
when my mind is full of
thoughts
and I don't know what to do.
My blessing from the LORD
had finally come to light,
but I ruined it with my
notions
and I made it go to flight.
My mind is in a battle
my heart is on the edge
anxieties at the forefront

My flesh has drawn a wedge.
But LORD, YOU know my
ways
and my thoughts before I do.
YOU know all my faults.
I don't know what else to do.
So I come to YOU in tears,
to pour out of my heart.
I don't know how to heal,
but you could show me where
to start.
I've destroyed all of YOUR
blessings,
and I've caused them all to
flee.
I didn't recognize YOUR
blessings,
and the fault lies with me.

10/18/09

If I Didn't Have Time For You

If I were to say, I'm too busy
to hear your earnest prayer;
And if I wasn't faithful and
never desired being there,
If I didn't have time to hear
when you're sick and want to
give in;
Ignoring your plea for
forgiveness to rid you of sin?

What If I had respect of
persons; gave favor to certain
ones?
Out of all the souls in the
world, you might've been the
left-out one.
If I put MY time before your
needs; disregarded all of your
dreams?
Didn't have time to become
your sins and give MY life to
redeem?

What would you say if I
didn't hear the smallest of
your desires?
If I didn't bring you out when
you're going through the
suffering fires?

If I used MY time for
pleasure; indulging while
ignoring your plea?
If you see where I am coming
from, why do you do these
things to ME?
Do you hear ME? You must
be faithful in order to see MY
face.
Are you listening? You must
be faithful to enter the HOLY
PLACE!
Get your priorities straight,
for I am soon to come!
And if you're busy still
putting ME last, you'll have
nowhere to run!

2003 Jessica Thomas
Inspired by the LORD JESUS

ONLY TO DRAW YOU

It's only to draw you closer, MY love
For you belong to ME.
The pain and hurt is only leading
To bliss you can't yet see.
I'm sorry it must be this way
To change your stony heart,
But I will surely bring you out!
I'm the POTTER; the epitome of art!
I'll spin, break and mold you;
Then place you in the fire,
Bring you forth, shiny and refined
As a vessel that's truly desired.
So, don't think you're losing the battle!
I am right beside you.
I feel everything you're going through
And if you let ME, I am here to guide you.
Then will your eyes be opened
And the veil will rip away!
Then you can shout that
I AM your GOD and with
ME you will always stay!

LET IT GO

Let it all go, and watch GOD move
You think its over, but GOD will prove
that faith is real, but requires an act
that shows that you know the unseen is fact
Trust that GOD can work it out
by destroying your way and denying the doubt
GOD won't work when you stand in the way
HIS hands are tied and tucked away
You say, *"Let it go? It'll all be lost.*
It's a gamble. I must count the cost."
But there's no choice if you want what's best
You can never lose if you pass this test.
So, give up the feelings, anxiety, and fear that
this matter is causing and be of good cheer.
Give it to JESUS and don't take it back!
When HE'S done, you will surely see the facts!

Written between June and Sept. 1, 2008
Inspired by the LORD JESUS
Written by Jessica B. Thomas

RACE FOR LIFE

As I run this race the devil's gaining on my track.
I slow down in my pace if I stop to look back.
So, I lay aside the weight that easily slows me down
And I ignore the devil's bait that he has placed on the ground.
As I decide to pick up speed, I begin to lose my breath
Though I felt it was a need to use the energy that was left.
I stop to pick a flower that is planted on the side
But it's a trick to steal the power GOD had given for the stride.
Friends who used to run, chose to run with me no more.
They were lured by temporal fun and say that running is a bore.
I was tempted to agree but it would surely slow my pace
So, I decide instead to flee. This is an individual race.
As I get closer to the goal and leave the slothful ones behind,
I run to save my soul and focus on the finish line.
But my legs would finally give, causing me to trip and fall,
But through the will to live, I gain the strength to crawl.
Through GOD, I drag and pull my way as others pass me by.
Yet, I must keep a steady pace, or cease the race and die.
Right before I reach my goal; right before the break of day,
Satan stands to take my soul, and proceeds to block my way.
I begin to call on JESUS who was with me all along,
And HE made the devil flee and sent him back where he belongs.
I regain GOD given strength to make it passed the line
where JESUS stands, and waits and I leave the world behind.

Given by JESUS CHRIST
Written by Jessica Thomas
Started 24 May 04 finished 2 July 04

RAFT

A raft on troubled waters
The waves are raging high
Holding for survival
Rolling thunder lines the sky
A thought invades the surface
"Give up and cease the fight!"
Deep down your hearts
reminded
somehow you'll be all right.
The wind is strong and
forceful
so, you're tossed into the sea
and the troubled waters
cover you
as the raft has set you free.
As you rise above the surface
embracing air to catch your
breath,
You search for missing pieces
grabbing hold to what is left
Feeling lost and lonely
no help at all in view.
All hope has been diminished
and your destiny lies
with you.
The storm appears so
powerful-
unyielding in its length
You fear you can't compare
against the power of its
strength
You regret leaving the shelter
to wander from the ark.
You never thought you'd do it
now you're lost out in the
dark.
At last! A glimpse of light
at your point of letting go.
The waves began to calm
and the winds began to slow.
Off into the distance
you see a glimpse of land.
and you look toward the sky
where JESUS stretches out
HIS hand.

Given by the LORD JESUS
Written by Jessica Thomas
May 05

STILL STANDING

YOU found me at my lowest
when I feared for my life
And then YOU picked me up
and paid the full price
YOU pulled me from the mire
and scrubbed away the mud;
saved my life from drowning
in the enemy's flood
There I was a babe; leaning on
the LORD
filled with much zeal and a
warrior's sword
But when the first windstorm
began to blow
and the rainstorm came, YOU
bid them to go
And I'm still standing because
of YOU
I called on YOUR name and
YOU always came through
As I journeyed along in this
tedious race
I felt that I could speed up in my
pace
Until a thunderstorm flowed
my way
I turned to run, but YOU bid me
to stay

There were lessons I had to learn
through the storm
but the fear grew the more when
the darker clouds formed
So YOU pulled me out like a
true-loving friend
YOU warned me to pray for I'll
face it again
And I'm still standing because
of YOU
I called on YOUR name and
YOU always came through
As time went on, I could
barely see,
because a great sandstorm was
blinding me
blocking the view of the
blessings YOU hold
Burying my faith; threatening
my soul
So I called on YOU to pull
me out
But YOU said, "Stay there and
get rid of the doubt!
In order to grow you must stay a
while longer
and when you come out your
faith will be stronger.

HOLD ON through this storm
and know I AM there!
A greater storm is coming. It is
here you prepare."
I rested and allowed YOU to
lead the way
I learned to let go; let YOU have
YOUR way
*And I'm still standing because
of YOU*
I called on YOUR name and
YOU brought me through
I felt I was seasoned and learned
all I could
When the wind started blowing,
I said, "It's all good."
And the rain started falling, I
knew what to do.
The thunder was like music; I
eased my way through.
When the sand started blowing,
I just put on my shades
And I told YOU, "Don't worry! I
got this thing made."
But something was strange and
fearfully new
The force became stronger the
more the wind blew
I planted my feet and buried my
fear
And remembered the lessons I'd
learned through the years
There it was, a category five
The "Hurricane of Fire" had
finally arrived

I remembered YOUR words, my
faithful FRIEND
Then I looked to the clouds at
the fierce whirlwind
It grew larger the more it
gathered the rain
And the louder it sounded, like
a rushing train
But YOU stood right there in
the tornado's path
and by faith, I knew it couldn't
stand YOUR wrath
The seas were roaring with
troubled waves
I started to stumble, but I knew
I was saved
Then I looked up to YOU and
held my breath
for I thought the Tsunami
would be my death.
Suddenly, the rains and the
winds ceased to blow
and the troubled waters were at
a calm flow
*And I was still standing because
of YOU*
I called on YOUR name and
YOU brought me through

TEMPEST

The storm comes and it's gloomy and dark
with winds, rain and lightning sparks.
A dreadful feeling of imminent destruction
and aftershocks of doubt and corruption.
Shouting waters deep and high,
strongly, violent on every side.
The comforts of life all washed away
so reliant before but a memory today.
Injuries from the flying debris
leaves permanent scars for others to see.
Fear is present and grips the heart
afraid of the clouds so fierce and dark.
So it is when trials and troubles come,
tolerant to few, unbearable to some.
Seeming to be no sign of relief
knowing satan has come in the form of a thief
to steal your joy, strength and endurance.
To make you give in to his tempting allurance.
But we must remember the LORD is there
no matter how dark or gloomy the air.
But hold on to GOD no matter the fear
Your sunshine will come. Restoration is near.

Finished 10 January 1998

WHEN I LET GO
TESTS AND TRIALS

Darkness turned to light
Everything was new
Rainclouds rolled away
Gray skies turned to blue

Thirsty soul was quenched
Sadness turned to glee
Tears were dried away
Chains broke off of me

09/14/10

YOUR FACE

I seek YOUR face
for answers; in trouble, in strife
YOU'RE the ultimate
in power, victory, and life
I call YOUR name
for safety; in danger, in need
And YOU will surely answer
To YOUR servant's cry indeed
I search for YOU
In darkness, confusion, and grief
YOU'RE right there in the midst
As I wait for YOUR relief
I wait for YOU
In patience, peace, in song
I know YOU hear my prayers
Therefore, it won't be long

Given by the LORD JESUS
Written by J. Thomas
08.14.04
Written at work/209 gate (in vehicle 266)
waiting for Tropical
Storm Charley to pass

CUSTOM WRITTEN
POEMS

A poem for Janis

There lives a mighty potter who took a piece of clay,
and formed a baby Janis in HIS own special way.
He already knew exactly how HE wanted her to be,
but it would take a long process to remove unwanted debris
See, HE had to remove the pride, shyness, fear, sin and self
before HE placed her in the fire and displayed her on the shelf.
so, HE began to mold Janis in the days of her youth;
placed her in situations to see if she'd tell the truth.
HE vowed to give her boldness which would take the longest time,
so, HE placed her on the table to guide her through the grind.
Janis was painfully shy throughout her time in school.
So, the potter pulled those pebbles with HIS special sculpting tool.
This would be a special vessel, which would take a little time
throughout the trials of life to come forth shiny and refined.
HE wedged the clay by hand to get out any extra air
then HE laid a foundation on the wheel that was prepared.
As the wheel would spin, HE gave her depth and height.
Then HE shaped her in HIS word that she would learn what's right.
She was place upon a shelf to dry her vessel from the spin;
to learn the word of GOD, to overcome her sin.
Once she was ready, HE trimmed and sponged the extra clay.
Then HE placed her on the shelf again until a later day.
Yet, all along HE watched her making sure she wouldn't crack.
HE knew how long to dry and when to take her off the rack.
She was placed into the fire, forcing out impurities
to prepare her for the glaze to take on CHRIST'S identity.

For Janis had to learn to stand up through her trials.
CHRIST was forming up her vessel as a minister all the while
before the glaze could be applied, he gave it one last look;
for if she couldn't stand the fire, he would blot her from the book.
So, he sanded away the bumps and smoothed the imperfections
providing a clean surface before he glazed her with perfection.
Then he dipped her in his blood and covered every part.
His glaze would give her liberty and soften up her heart.
When she was set aside to dry, she felt he didn't care
even though she couldn't feel him; JESUS stayed right there.
Once the time had come, the vessel had to mature,
so, he returned her to the fire at the highest temperature.
He left her in the kiln so she could slowly cool.
So, his work would be complete, and he could use her as his tool.

Thank you,
JESUS
completed Aug. 9, 2006
Written for my sister Janis

For Jennifer, 11/25/15

Through many dangers, toils, and snares,
You've already come
You are stronger than you believe
And a subtle guide to some

From a bud into a rose
You've matured through many storms,
disappointments, aches and pains.
Life has forced you to conform.

Your thorns were only steps
That will lift you from the dirt.
Everything you lost in life
GOD pruned to take away the hurt.

Your fragrance fills the air
As the SON helps you to grow,
And the fears you hide inside
Only GOD and you will know.

Yet, time continues on
But your rose shall never fade
If you hold on through life's test
And let GOD's pruning pave the way.

jbt

GREATER HORIZONS

TIME WILL NOT PASS QUIETLY ALONG,
SO, IT GRABS A HOLD AND LEADS US ON
TO HIGHER HEIGHTS TOO FAR TO SEE
IT ENSLAVES US, REFUSING TO SET US FREE

THOUGH WE FIGHT WITH ALL THE POWER WITHIN
OUR FIGHT IS IN VAIN. TIME ALWAYS WINS
SO, RELAX AND ALLOW IT TO CARRY YOU THROUGH
TO THE GREATER HORIZONS AWAITING YOU

TIME WAITS FOR NONE BUT IS JOYFUL AND FREE
IT KNOWS WHAT'S AHEAD; WHERE
OUR EYES CAN'T SEE
AS TIME NOW APPROACHES YOUR OPEN DOOR
TO CARRY YOU HIGHER; TO BLESS YOU WITH MORE,
RELAX AND ALLOW IT TO LEAD YOU THROUGH
FOR TIME ALWAYS KNOWS WHAT'S BEST FOR YOU.

HAPPY RETIREMENT,
TO MY CO-WORKER GARRIS
WRITTEN BY JESSICA B. THOMAS
(TO GOD BE THE GLORY)
03-03-2006

I PRAYED FOR YOU, a wedding poem

I prayed for you when I was lonely and when I needed a friend.
I prayed when my past relationships suddenly came to an end.
I longed for you when I noticed couples happy and holding hands.
But I knew that GOD had promised this day, so all I could do was stand.
Satan placed many false blessings within my view,
But my sacrifice of faith only cleared the path for you.
I prayed for you at times my heart utterly bled with despair.
When it seem this day would never come and only GOD cared.
But look what GOD has done! We're walking down the aisle!
Ready to make a vow to GOD and each other as we smile.
A vow that means I'll love your forever, my precious Love. For life!
A life that can only be fulfilled and complete with JESUS CHRIST.
As I speak my vows, I mean each and every word.
For I know that in the presence of the LORD they are heard.
I say them from my heart and deep down within my soul.
GOD prepared both you and I to forever have and to hold.
I prayed for you, my love, our lives have just begun.
May GOD allow us to grow old together and to always live as one.

I WAS THERE

I know that you are angry but I was there.

All the time, in the midst, I was there.

Though you ignored when I called, I offered you MY all.

Some refused and disbelieved, but I was there.

When the towers gave way, I was there

And the five sides collapsed in despair.

As the Eagle's heart tore and the Nation cried, "War"

And the armies marched on, I was there.

When your prayers weren't prayed, I was there.

When you never came to ME with your cares.

As you cried all through the night; how I longed to make it right.

Standing back with open arms, I was there.

When you blamed ME for the evil. I stayed there.

You asked where was MY presence; why didn't I care?

As the flames steady burned and for answers your heart yearned.

When the darkness covered goodness, I stayed there.

When the smoke began to clear, you saw ME there.

Through the hands of all the people who showed they cared.

The divided began to unite and the separate and loose grew tight.

When the Nation stood the "storm," you saw ME there.

The enemy will not prevail for I am there.

As you turned and cried MY name, I heard your prayers.

When the wounds began to heal and numb hearts again could feel remember ME for I AM near; I'M always there!

Given by the LORD JESUS
Written by Jessica Thomas
Sept. 2001

122

Leah!

I waited for my time; for the one who's right for me.
It seemed to take a while as if that day would never be.
But when my Jacob came to town, my heart leaped hard inside.
When I saw his body's frame, all my tact was pushed aside.
He was only being kind when introduced to me,
cause when my sister came along, she was all that he could see.
I tried to play it off, as if I didn't know.
Maybe if I make him laugh, his love for her would go.
If I change my hair or change the clothes I wear;
If I paint my tender eyes; add flowers to my hair,
he would love me then, and forget about the rest.
If I change the way I am, he would see that I'm the best.
Yet, she remained the same; didn't have to change a thing.
She was free to be herself and he wants her to wear his ring.
She makes me feel undone, because he looks at her in love,
but he deals with me in pity when she's the one he's thinking of.
So, I resort to other means to win his heart's affection.
Though she's the one he wants, I'm next in the election.
So, I'll wait until he's drunk and I'll enter into his tent.
I'll don the wedding veil that he can't see who's really sent.
For a moment, I'll be his and he'll be free to have his way,
but when he awakens to my face, I can't imagine what he'd say.
That night would seal his fate and I'd have him to myself:
Seven years of toil and labor. Maybe now I am worth the wealth.
Even though I planned and schemed, his heart was never there,
but when Rachel came along, songs of joy were everywhere.
So, he desired Rachel; I was just an average Jill.
It's hard for him to love me. I don't feel he ever will.
Through all the love and children, I thought he'd changed his mind.
Fourteen years of toil for Rachel and my love was left behind.
You see, I tried to make him love me, but that's impossible to do.
I had to learn this lesson so I could share today with you.
If someone doesn't love you, don't try to make it so!
Give your hopes to JESUS and let those feelings go!

Influence: Genesis 29

LOVE OF A LIFETIME

If I had a thousand more years
to express my love to you,
it wouldn't be enough.
Just a glimpse and then it's through
It would be as just one day
I'd get to hold you once again.
Show you that I love you,
Before that day would end.

Our love was like a dream
others pray a lifetime for.
My dream will never end.
You remain forever more.
Love of my lifetime
Joyce, you were to me.
Ever on my mind.
With you I long to be.

Life is like a vapor
That quickly fades away.
Never did I think goodbye
Would come to me that day.
I still hear your laughter,
Smell your fragrance,
see your face, and I
hear you call my name.
Just one more embrace.

I have known you most of life.
It's unbelievable that you're gone.
My heart is skipping beats
When I hear our favorite song
And in our favorite places,
My heart aches just the more.
I miss your smiling face
"Ti amo, mi amor." (I love you, my love)

For Andy and Joyce
Inspiration: Andy's love
For Joyce
JBT 2016

THEY CALL ME RED

I walk the color red
Therefore, I must be strong
Though hurtful things are said,
I continue to walk along
Wrapped in crimson stain
GOD introduced HIS love
Sheltered me from rain
Birthed me from above
See, I felt that I was fine
Before GOD pulled me out
In my darkness HIS light shined
As I stumbled along death's route
Yet, HE was always there
Though I ignored HIS constant plea
HIS signs were everywhere
And HE wouldn't let me be
I walk the color red
For someone prayed for me
When in my life was dread
GOD came to set me free.
My five stars held their breath
As the sun and moon eclipsed
He almost caused my death
Yet, through pain, now I'm equipped
To walk the color red
Though some don't understand

They counted me as dead
But my life was in GOD'S hand
As the hourglass loosed its grains
CHRIST pulled me from the storm
HE took all of my pain
And used it to conform
I can stand against the giants
Through the trials I am made strong
Against all evil, I stand defiant
Of this world, I don't belong
For now I'm covered in the red
My life is not my own
The old lifestyle is dead
And I will never walk alone.

Written for my Sister Cheryl Phillips (Red)
Jan. 17, 2014
Cheryl is the mother of five children.
She lived through Domestic Violence.
The LORD rescued her!

TO BE WITH YOU

To hear your voice is music
That soothes my restless
mind.
It makes my heart beat
stronger
To break the chain that binds.

To feel your gentle kiss
make the passion overflow.
Just to rest in your embrace
Makes my longing for you
grow.

Your eyes are filled with
laughter
Like an Angel's eyes
would be.
I get caught up in the moment
When your eyes are
reflecting me.

Time passes by so quickly
when I'm spending it
with you.
Yet the more I'm in your
presence,
The more I feel brand-new.

I could live and breathe your
love
And never leave your touch.
No other woman appeals
to me,
I feel for you that much.

Of course, we have our days,
But true love always prevails.
We can mend the broken
pieces
For with GOD, we'll never
fail.

Written for a friend of mine
to give to his wife/girlfriend
2003

WE RETURN TO YOU

Sept. 11, 2001 dedication.

We return to YOU, though tragedy leads the way
We, like sheep, were all gone astray
Denied YOUR existence, replaced with our own.
Left the Bible, the churches, and prayer all alone
YOU'VE knocked on our doors when the weather was cold
We peeped through the opening and walked away bold
Though the rain, the sleet, and snow gathered ground
YOU continued to knock though no one was around
We've laid YOU aside and worshipped another
Indulged in the flesh, making sin our lover
Then suddenly, in the sky, a tragedy took place
As we looked the hills with fear on our face
Unbelievable it seemed as the towers gave way
Never dreamed as a nation we'd come to this day
This tragedy has touched everyone who could view
With our tears and our prayers, we all looked to YOU
YOU LORD, who's been there through our daily routine
As we rose up to play; placed YOU last on the scene
We come to YOU humbled, our heads bowed low
Asking forgiveness for the sins we had sown
We prepare our armies and plead YOUR guiding LIGHT
To lead us on to victory and with YOUR weapons, fight.

Inspired by the LORD JESUS
influence: 9-11
Written by Jessica Thomas

WHEN THE DAY IS THROUGH

In the hustle and toil of
the day,
when my mind is clogged
with tasks,
and figuring out a way, or
who I'm going to ask
that'll make my day go
smooth
and the burdens a little light
when I'm always on the move
and nothing's going right.

Yet, no one understands
and nothing seems to aid,
I stand, a desperate man
as the daylight slowly fades

So, I'll look to GOD and wait.
HE'S where my help comes
from.
HE'LL relieve me of the
weights
so that my soul will not
succumb
to the pressures of the day.
GOD will set my mind at ease
until the darkness goes away
and, again, I freely breathe.

And when my day is through
I'll release the deepest sigh,
and I'll sit upon my bike
and ride off into the sky

To Marion T. Davis
Inspired by GOD for you
Written by J. Thomas
07/09/2007

YOU LEAVE BEHIND A LIGHT

You must've been an angel and GOD had given me to you
For such a time as life where in a moment it is through
Time seems to me so short when life proves to be so good
Never dreamed this day would be, yet I knew one day it would
So soon your shadow faded, yet it leaves behind a light
That reminds me of your goodness as
your spirit takes its flight
You must've been an angel, and your mission was complete
To bring me peace and joy-to make my bitter moments sweet
I'll miss your kind heart, the way you
laughed; I miss your smile
My heart, now filled with sorrow, will be peaceful in a while,
because you leave behind a light as I
recall the things you've done.
That light will glow in radiance; warming all just like the sun.
As my heavy heart grows lighter and my tears are dried away,
The LORD will make me stronger as
I journey through the day
You will live on in my memories, my laughter, and my tears
As I continue on in life, reminiscing through the years.

Written by Jessica Thomas
Inspired by the LORD JESUS

CPSIA information can be obtained
at www.ICGtesting.com
Printed in the USA
BVHW032250250419
546615BV00001B/42/P